SEED Pack 2

Priscilla Shirer

LifeWay Press®
Nashville, Tennessee

ISBN 9781415871355
Item 005442090

Dewey Decimal Classification: 248.84
Subject Heading: HABIT \ SPIRITUAL WARFARE \ SPIRITUAL LIFE

To order additional copies of this resource, write to LifeWay Church Resources Customer Service; One LifeWay Plaza, Nashville, TN 37234-0013; fax (615) 251-5933; call toll free (800) 458-2772; e-mail orderentry@lifeway.com; order online at www. lifeway.com; or visit the LifeWay Christian Store serving you.

Published in the United States of America

Leadership and Adult Publishing
LifeWay Church Resources
One LIfeWay Plaza
Nashville, TN 37234-0175

contents

about the author

PRISCILLA SHIRER is a wife and mom first but put a Bible
in her hand and a message in her heart and you'll see why
thousands meet God in powerful, personal ways through her
resources and conferences. Through the expository teaching of
God's Word, Priscilla's desire is to see women not only know the
uncompromising truths of Scripture intellectually but also to
experience them practically by the power of the Holy Spirit.

Priscilla is a graduate of Dallas Theological Seminary and the
author of several books and Bible studies including *A Jewel In
His Crown, Discerning the Voice of God,* and *One in a Million.*
She and her husband, Jerry, lead Going Beyond Ministries from
their hometown of Dallas, Texas, never too far from their three
growing boys.

www.goingbeyond.com

WAIT!
Don't turn the page yet.
I've gotta talk to you first.

I'm so glad you're joining me. I love Bible study. Anyone who knows me can attest to that. Since you have this book in your hand, I'm assuming you love it too. Yet I've often wondered if, in our desire to dig deeply into the treasure of God's Word, we may be missing one of the most critical and stunning realities of our relationship with the Bible: God speaks not only to shape our theology but to mold our current reality.

You see, I'll admit that I'm hooked on theology. The mere sight of a bookshelf filled with Bible commentaries makes my breath catch. Yet amidst the commentaries, Bible research software, and scholarly data that I would always encourage you to benefit from, God's own Spirit began to whisper sweetly to me, asking me to come to Him with nothing open except His Word and my heart, ready to hear His voice and to experience the living, active power of the Scriptures. Armed with this new objective, God prompted me to make certain my devotional time was as rich as my Bible study time.

To be clear: I'm not suggesting that we disregard the amazing resources we've been offered to help us rightly divide the Word of truth. I'm only suggesting that we not neglect the powerful experience of meditating on God's Word in the process. If you have felt the same stirring, we have designed this resource to assist.

Prepare yourself, my friend. This resource will most likely be different from the last study you had in your hands. You won't find mounds of documented insights or words researched in their original form for meaning. Nor have I provided the amount of application questions you'd normally expect from something I'd write. While I've occasionally included some help and worked hard to be certain we use passages in context, I purposely designed this study to lead you back to personal meditation, prayerful observation, and listening to God's Spirit as He seeks to illumine Scripture.

If you feel a bit of hesitation (that maybe you should grab your receipt and head back to the bookstore rather than grab a pen), I urge you to turn the first page and dive in. Any reluctance you feel is understandable. In our highly blessed culture where we have Bible study resources at our immediate disposal, we've become a bit handicapped and ... can I say it ... lazy. We like the work being done by someone more "capable," more "spiritual," more ... ahhh, you fill in the blank. But you, my friend, are filled with God's Spirit. He is ready to be your personal tour guide through the Word. So don't quit before you've even started. I think you will be surprised with the outcome.

How this resource works

At the beginning of each week you'll read an article and watch a video session, if you've decided to get the video. You can use this workbook without the video. Both the article and video will present a theme for you to consider before the Lord for the remainder of that week. Then each week I've given you Scripture to consider that complements the theme. You will notice that we've given you 10 passages per subject. Choose one daily, and give it your attention. If you do one per day, you could start the study all over again and have more verses to study on the same themes.

I'm asking you to use the following principles in your devotional time. I call them the "Five P's of Hearing God Through the Bible." They have revolutionized my quiet time, and I'm excited to share them with you. When you've chosen the passage you want to concentrate on, apply these principles.

The Five P's

1. Position Yourself to Hear from God
Engage in solitude and silence, and approach the text with anticipation, expecting God to speak to you.

2. Pore Over the Passage and Paraphrase the Major Points

Don't just skim the passage. Take your time and meditate on it (Josh. 1:8). Read the passage a few times, emphasizing different words in the verse each time. If a certain word or phrase speaks to you, don't ignore it. Stop and consider why it is meaningful. This is how the Spirit speaks. He connects Scripture to the details of our lives.

If the passage allows, put yourself in the Scripture and see yourself in the story. If one verse seems to resonate with you, don't worry about finishing the rest—just stay in the passage, and let the Spirit speak to you. As you meditate on Scripture, consider the context. What takes place both before and after the passage?

After you've meditated on the verse(s), use the space we've given you to paraphrase each verse. In just one or two simple sentences, summarize what is happening. These questions might help you to get the most out of each verse selection as you pore over the passage:

- Who are the major participants?
- What are they doing? saying?
- Where are they going?

3. Pull Out the Spiritual Principles

Close your Bible and look at your paraphrases. For each one, spiritualize the major point. What is God teaching? What is He revealing about Himself? Is there a command to be followed? Is there a promise to be regarded? Write them down.

4. Pose the Question
Turn each spiritual principle that you listed in the step above into a personally directed question. Ask yourself questions that will help you come to these conclusions:

- Am I living in a way that coincides with the message of this verse?
- Is anything in my life contradicting this passage?
- What do I need to do to bring my life in line with this verse?

As you sit in God's presence with these questions, record what you begin to hear the Spirit encouraging you, convicting you, challenging you, or inspiring you to do.

5. Plan Obedience and Pin Down a Date
Determine the steps you can take to immediately begin responding to what God has said to you, and put them into practice immediately. If obedience requires you to do something specific, record a date and time you will follow through. Let someone else know about your plan so you can be held accountable.

A Personal Example
Here's an illustration from my personal journal from several years ago on how these principles assisted me to have a meaningful conversation with God. I was reading John 1:36-37. "[John the Baptist] looked at Jesus as He walked, and said, 'Behold, the Lamb of God!' The two disciples heard him speak, and they followed Jesus" (NASB).

After positioning myself to hear from God—the first P—and having nothing but my Bible, journal, and hot cup of tea nearby, I continued with the remaining 4 P's.

Pore and Paraphrase
- Verse 36: John's eyes were on Jesus. John's ministry was focused on pointing out the Lamb of God.

- Verse 37: John's message resulted in an increased desire in the listeners to follow hard after Jesus.

Pull
- Verse 36: True ministry means the minister's eyes are focused on Jesus. True ministry should call all attention only to the Lamb of God.

- Verse 37: True ministry should encourage those who hear to desire an intimate personal experience with Jesus more than a relationship with the minister.

Pose
- Verse 36: Are my eyes focused on Jesus or some-one/something else? If so, what? Do I seek to call attention only to the Lamb of God, or do I seek any for myself?

- Verse 37: When people hear my message, do they want more of me or are they encouraged to seek hard after Him?

Purpose and Pin
- When I teach Bible study and in ministry from this day forward, I must develop messages that focus the listener only on seeing Jesus.
- How can I tweak my message to reflect this goal?
- My intention should not be to call attention to myself in any way.
- I want to begin to see people's interest stirred to experience more of God and less of me after hearing me speak.

On this day I was stunned as the searchlight of God's personal Word to me profoundly penetrated my heart. With His conviction through these two simple verses, the Spirit began redirecting the course of my entire ministry. I am a testament to the fact that God speaks through His Word and what He will say can indeed change the course of your very life.

I have no doubt that if you will utilize the "5 P's" you will marvel at the clarity with which you will begin to hear God. He's ready to speak if we'll just tune in to listen! I don't want to miss one word He has to say, and I'm certain that neither do you.

Are you ready?
Let's go.

Priscilla

SESSION 1

STAGE FRIGHT

DVD SESSION: ARMOR

> "For our battle is not against flesh and blood, but against the rulers, against the authorities, against the world powers of this darkness, against the forces of evil in the heavens."
> —Ephesians 6:12, HCSB

The tiny hairs on the nape of my neck stood at attention. My cold and clammy palms twitched rhythmically. My chest felt burdened as if it might suffocate under the pressure of the mound of escalating, odious emotion. I'd seen this side of myself before. It had appeared on several other occasions when Fear had shown up at the door and barged his way in. He'd curled up beside me, along with his twin brother Intimidation who'd slipped in almost unnoticed. He put his feet up on the coffee table beside my teaching notes.

He stared at them.

I stared at him.

Then his eyes caught mine long enough for him to see behind their glassy surface and deep into the depths of my heart. The smirk curling at the end of his crooked jaw made me look away, ashamed.

Now he knew for sure that he'd gotten to me, just like he did the last time.

As if on cue, Fear took off his coat and sauntered across the room to hang it on the hook in the corner. He kicked off his shoes and then cracked his knuckles like a pianist limbering up for a masterful musical rendition. He grabbed my hand and intertwining my fingers into his, he whispered, "We're here to stay a while."

I hung my head. I couldn't believe they were here. Again. Like the pushy guests they are, Fear and Intimidation had invited themselves over. I felt violated; yet as always, I was too upset to realize the power I had to send them away.

That was the way this saga always played out for me, and their intrusions were getting worse. These visitors didn't show up on rare occasion anymore, like in-laws popping over for a surprise visit during the holidays. They'd moved in, carrying all the baggage that guests like these always do.

This time, as I sat there, slowly sinking into an oversized sofa tucked in a dimly lit green room just off stage, they refused to realize that they'd long worn out their welcome.

Some have called this stage fright. I call it sheer terror.

I had prepared a message to deliver to the 2,000+ women who had gathered, and I could hear the group roar with laughter and applause as they prepared to receive me. This was a great group, sitting on the edge of their seats ready to hear from God. Yet I was nothing short of terrified to walk out on the platform. My stomach churned like the old ice cream maker my momma would pull out on hot summer days. My legs wobbled, and my breath became shallow. The knot in my throat was so tightly strung I thought it'd take a clever magician to unravel it.

I was sure that my normally booming voice would never reach clarity once I stepped in front of these precious women. To be honest, I didn't know for sure that I wouldn't make a run for it once that solitary beam of the spot light illumined my presence in the otherwise blackened auditorium.

(Note to self: Check for the nearest exits.)

I saw a survey somewhere that said people feared public speaking more than death itself. I laughed the first time I read it. I couldn't fathom the notion of someone volunteering for the guillotine just to avoid facing a spotlight and a crowd. Now, somehow, I was fully convinced. I'd opt for the noose.

This event marked a series of similar instances over the course of six months during which I endured the most grueling battle against fear I have faced in my life. At this point, I'd been a speaker for almost a decade, and yet someway, somehow, fear had begun to grip me with an unfamiliar intensity.

At first I thought I'd just get over it, but then time passed and I realized that this mountain was both too high and too steep for even the most skilled climber to scale. I called a mentor for direction. He wisely informed me that this kind of fear (the kind that refuses to leave) was not a mere emotion to deal with but a spiritual stronghold to demolish. Unless I fought for my freedom, I'd find the bondage would only continue.

I prepared for war and went to the battlefield in spiritual armor. Scripture became my offensive weapon to fight against the enemy of my soul for territory he was trying desperately to win. The lies that were paralyzing me had to be replaced by God's truth. I literally spoke God's Word to myself until I changed my own mind.

I was tired of Fear and Intimidation ringing my doorbell at all hours of the day or night and leaving their footprints across my floor. The more I struggled, the more I realized they were on assignment from an enemy who's always been working to keep me from my God-given destiny. The enemy wanted the guillotine for God's destiny for my life.

And he wants the same for you.
He seeks to get you so comfortable keeping house with his two favorite intruders that you'll be too busy keeping up with them to notice what they're keeping from you. Without recognizing the demonic strategy, many of us shrink back in despair and allow Fear and Intimidation to have their way with us.

Before we know it, we have abandoned our calling and traded in the abundant life for a mundane one.

It's time to send these unwanted guests packing. They may still knock, but we can refuse to let them in. No more stage fright for us. We're walking onto the center stage of God's will—smack dab in the middle of God's purposes.

This doesn't mean we won't have butterflies anymore. It does mean now they'll at least fly in formation. We've got new guests to entertain. The Competence and Adequacy that come directly from God's Spirit (2 Cor. 3:5-6) are ready to make our acquaintance. No more excuses, and no more fear. I'm ready for God's best. You too? Then quit standing back there looking for the nearest exit. Get moving! The stage of God's plan is divinely lit just for you, and a crowd of people need what you're offering.

1 SAMUEL 17:23-26 (NIV)

As David was talking with his brothers

"Goliath, the Philistine champion from Gath, stepped out from his lines and shouted his usual defiance, and David heard it. When the Israelites saw the man, they all ran from him in great fear. Now the Israelites had been saying, 'Do you see how this man keeps coming out? He comes out to defy Israel. The king will give great wealth to the man who kills him. He will also give him his daughter in marriage and will exempt his father's family from taxes in Israel.'
David asked the men standing near him, 'What will be done for the man who kills this Philistine and removes this disgrace from Israel? Who is this uncircumcised Philistine that he should defy the armies of the living God?'"

position

pore & paraphrase

pull

pose

plan

2 TIMOTHY 1:6-7 (HCSB)

"Therefore, I remind you to keep ablaze the gift of God that is in you through the laying on of my hands. For God has not given us a spirit of fearfulness, but one of power, love, and sound judgment."

position

pore & paraphrase

pull

pose

plan

"Keep ablaze—(or perhaps, 'keep at full flame') his God-given ability for ministry. God's gifts must be used if they are to reach and maintain their full potential."[1]

Laying on of hands was used for ordination, the act of officially investing someone with religious authority.

2 KINGS 6:15-17 (NLT)

"When the servant of the man of God got up early the next morning and went outside, there were troops, horses, and chariots everywhere . 'Oh, sir, what will we do now?' the young man cried out to Elisha. 'Don't be afraid!' Elisha told him. 'For there are more on our side than on theirs!' Then Elisha prayed, 'O LORD, open his eyes and let him see!' The LORD opened the young man's eyes, and when he looked up, he saw that the hillside around Elisha was filled with horses and chariots of fire."

"In the fear of the Lord, there is strong confidence and his children will have refuge" (Prov. 14:26).

"So that we can confidently say, 'The Lord is my helper, I will not be afraid. What will man do to me?'" (Heb. 13:6, NASB).

Horses and chariots of fire are a reference to the fiery agents of God.

ISAIAH 50:7-9 (NLT)

"Because the Sovereign LORD helps me, I will not be dismayed. Therefore, I have set my face like a stone, determined to do his will. And I know that I will not be put to shame. He who gives me justice is near.
Who will dare to bring charges against me now? Where are my accusers? Let them appear! See, the Sovereign LORD is on my side! Who will declare me guilty?
All my enemies will be destroyed like old clothes that have been eaten by moths!"

position

pore & paraphrase

pull

pose

plan

ZECHARIAH 4:6-7 (NASB)

"Then he said to me, 'This is the word of the LORD
to Zerubbabel saying, "Not by might nor by power,
but by My Spirit," says the LORD of hosts.
"What are you, O great mountain? Before Zerubbabel you
will become a plain; and he will bring forth the top stone
with shouts of 'Grace, grace to it!"' "

Zerubbabel was governor of Judah and leader of the building project to reconstruct the temple.

The "mountain" is a figurative expression to denote the various difficulties that stood in Zerubbabel's way and impeded the carrying out of his great design.

The bringing forth of the "top stone" (capstone) was most likely a metaphor to signify the completion of the work.

1 PETER 4:10-11 (NASB)

"As each one has received a special gift, employ it in serving one another as good stewards of the manifold grace of God. Whoever speaks, is to do so as one who is speaking the utterances of God; whoever serves is to do so as one who is serving by the strength which God supplies; so that in all things God may be glorified through Jesus Christ, to whom belongs the glory and dominion forever and ever. Amen."

"Gift" is from the Greek word charisma, *which is a favor one receives without any merit of his own. The gift of divine grace.*

A steward is one who has no wealth of his own but manages what he has at the direction of his master.

JUDGES 6:12-16 (NASB)

The Call of Gideon

"The angel of the LORD appeared to him and said to him, 'The LORD is with you, O valiant warrior.' Then Gideon said to him, 'O my lord, if the LORD is with us, why then has all this happened to us? And where are all His miracles which our fathers told us about, saying, "Did not the LORD bring us up from Egypt?" But now the LORD has abandoned us and given us into the hand of Midian.' The LORD looked at him and said, 'Go in this your strength and deliver Israel from the hand of Midian. Have I not sent you?' He said to Him, 'O Lord, how shall I deliver Israel? Behold, my family is the least in Manasseh, and I am the youngest in my father's house.' But the LORD said to him, 'Surely I will be with you, and you shall defeat Midian as one man.'"

The angel of the Lord described Gideon as a "valiant warrior" even though he was anything but that at this encounter.

Consider the excuses Gideon made to the Lord. Prayerfully consider excuses you've been prone to make.

2 CORINTHIANS 12:9-10 (AMP)

"But He [the Lord] said to me [Paul], My grace (My favor and loving-kindness and mercy) is enough for you [sufficient against any danger and enables you to bear the trouble manfully]; for My strength and power are made perfect (fulfilled and completed) and show themselves most effective in [your] weakness. Therefore, I will all the more gladly glory in my weaknesses and infirmities, that the strength and power of Christ (the Messiah) may rest (yes, may pitch a tent over and dwell) upon me! So for the sake of Christ, I am well pleased and take pleasure in infirmities, insults, hardships, persecutions, perplexities and distresses; for when I am weak [in human strength], then am I [truly] strong (able, powerful in divine strength)."

position

pore & paraphrase

pull

pose

plan

JEREMIAH 1:6-9 (NASB)

*Jeremiah's response after being called
by God to be a prophet*

"Then I said, 'Alas, Lord God! Behold, I do not know how to speak, Because I am a youth.' But the LORD said to me, 'Do not say, "I am a youth," Because everywhere I send you, you shall go, And all that I command you, you shall speak. Do not be afraid of them, For I am with you to deliver you,' declares the LORD. Then the LORD stretched out His hand and touched my mouth, and the LORD said to me, 'Behold, I have put My words in your mouth.'"

In the original language the phrase "too young" would have come from a word that can refer to an infant or young boy. Jeremiah was likely in his late teens or early twenties but was communicating that he felt like a baby in his level of experience and therefore ill-equipped for public ministry.

Make special note of the three major assurances God gave the hesitant prophet.

MATTHEW 25:14-15,16-29 (NASB)

"It is just like a man about to go on a journey, who called his own slaves and entrusted his possessions to them. To one he gave five talents, to another, two, and to another, one, each according to his own ability ... Immediately the one who had received the five talents went and traded with them, and gained five more talents. In the same manner the one who had received the two talents gained two more. But he who received the one talent went away, and dug a hole in the ground and hid his master's money. Now after a long time the master ... came and settled accounts with them. The one who had received the five talents ... brought five more talents, saying, 'Master, you entrusted five talents to me. See, I have gained five more.' His master said to him, 'Well done, good and faithful slave. You were faithful with a few things, I will put you in charge of many things ; enter into the joy of your master.' Also the one who had received the two talents came up and said, 'Master, you entrusted two talents to me. See, I have gained two more talents.' His master said to him, 'Well done, good and faithful slave. You were faithful with a few things, I will put you in charge of many things; enter into the joy of your master.'"

(continued)

A talent was a variable unit of weight and money used in ancient Greece, Rome, and the Middle East. In Hebrew weights it was equivalent to 3,000 shekels.

And the one also who had received the one talent came up and said, 'Master, I knew you to be a hard man, reaping where you did not sow and gathering where you scattered no seed. And I was afraid, and went away and hid your talent in the ground. See, you have what is yours.' But his master answered and said to him, 'You wicked, lazy slave, you knew that I reap where I did not sow and gather where I scattered no seed. Then you ought to have put my money in the bank, and on my arrival I would have received my money back with interest. Therefore take away the talent from him, and give it to the one who has the ten talents. For to everyone who has, more shall be given, and he will have an abundance; but from the one who does not have, even what he does have shall be taken away.'"

position

pore & paraphrase

pull

pose

plan

MORE SEEDS
Proverbs 28:1; Philippians 4:13; Isaiah 40:29; Matthew 25:14-30; 1 Corinthians 3:9-15;
Luke 19:11; Romans 8:31; Ephesians 1:16-20; Psalm 22:23; Luke 19:13; Ephesians 6:10; 2 Corinthians 13:4

LEASHES BREAK
AND DOGS BITE

> **"Sin is crouching at the door; and its desire is for you, but you must master it."**
> —Genesis 4:7, NASB

The morning was crisp and cool—perfect for a bike ride. I jumped out of bed around 7 a.m., dressed in an oversized sweatshirt and jogging pants, and bolted out the back door. I had 30 minutes to be alone and ease into the day before my house became alive with the chatter of little ones. Anxious to get some exercise and spend a few valued moments talking with the Lord, I headed down the normal route through my old neighborhood, a collage of brick homes, sidewalks, and mature trees.

Nothing new about the path that day. I passed the same houses and the same driverless cars warming up for their owners on the tree-lined streets. When I rounded the final corner to head down the last stretch of road, I fully expected to see the man who had become a familiar fixture during my bike rides. Same time and same place, I'd pass this gentleman walking his two beautiful dogs: one black and one brown.

We'd grown used to our interchange, and each of us always did what was necessary. When I saw them, I'd immediately cross the street, and he'd stop to wait for me to pass. The owner would wind the leash tightly around his hand and pull back to restrain the black dog. For some reason, that one didn't like me—or anyone else for that matter. Any person or object, living or inanimate, was subject to his cruel tantrums. While the gentle brown one didn't seem to notice me or care, the black one became vicious at the sight of me. He'd lunge in my direction and snarl with an open mouth full of sharp teeth.

I wasn't afraid. I'd grown used to this and appreciated my neighbor for being so trustworthy and polite in restraining that wild beast. Every day the same drill: I passed by while the dog barked in hopes of making an attack. I was sure this morning would be no different.

On this day the pleasantries between my neighbor and me were the same: the smile, the wave, the "good morning." I began to cross the street to take my usual place on the other side while he pulled back on his livid dog. I didn't glance back at them until I was on the opposite sidewalk, and when I did, I saw a sight I wasn't prepared for. The crazed animal had lunged at me with so much force that his leash snapped, breaking at the base. The dog was loose and racing feverishly across the street in my direction.

I began screaming at the top of my lungs as terror gripped my heart. I tried to speed up, but he was almost on my side of the road before I'd even realized he was coming. My feet kept pumping the pedals, but for some odd reason, I became strangely paralyzed. My right foot slipped off the worn rubber pad, and the bike tilted as I tried to hold steady. I swerved violently and came crashing down on the sidewalk just in time to come face to face with the dog that had rushed at me despite his owner's frantic calls.

In an instant he lunged into my thigh, tearing through my jogging pants and taking out a small piece of flesh. He continued barking and terrorizing me for only a few more seconds before my neighbor finally made it across the road, tackling his dog to the ground. It seemed like an eternity had passed. Bike in hand, I limped the rest of the way home.

Shouldn't I have known that at some point something like this was bound to happen? Leashes break, and dogs like this one eventually bite. How long could I pass by this animal and not expect to get into some trouble? Why did it take a frightening exchange and a hurtful bite to get me to realize that being this close to danger isn't worth it? I should have chosen a new path long before this day ever arrived.

Why do I ... why do _we_ play with fire?
Do we really think the flimsy restraints and leashes we've put in place will keep holding up?

Nothing is new under the sun because Joseph learned this lesson long ago. He had a normal routine just like me. "Day after day" (Gen. 39:10) he found himself in the same place at the same time participating in the same activity—overseeing his employer's personal wealth and fortune. From the early morning hours until the ones late in the day, his charge was to manage everything Potiphar owned. Joseph was trusted and had access to everything that Potiphar held dear.

Yet soon a dog started barking, and it couldn't be ignored. Potiphar's wife lusted for Joseph and began to request that he look after more than just her husband's wealth. He saw the danger but did not act appropriately until it was too late. With the barking dog still in sight on the next sidewalk—yet with good and honest intentions each day—he played with fire. Day after day he refused to compromise while hoping the leash would hold fast. Yet the dog barked, showing its sharp teeth more and more. (See Gen. 39:7-8.) Then one morning the leash broke.

"Now it happened one day that he went into the house to do his work, and none of the men of the household was there inside. She caught him by his garment saying, 'Lie with me!' And he left his garment in her hand and fled, and went outside. When she saw that he had left his garment in her hand and fled outside …Then she spoke to [her master] with these words, 'The Hebrew slave, whom you brought to us, came in to me to make sport of me; and as I raised my voice and screamed, he left his garment beside me and fled outside'" (Gen. 39:11-13,17-18, NASB).

With one swift lie, Potiphar's wife took a huge bite out of Joseph's reputation and his future. He was fired from his job and sentenced to a stint behind bars.

If only he'd run sooner. How his life would have been different had he chosen to walk down a different path!

Leashes break, and dogs bite. You can only walk down a road so close to that ferocious beast for so long before you are shocked by the position you find yourself in. Don't play with fire whatever your fire may be—the flirtatious glances, the Internet site, the seductive temptation. It will not be too long before you wish you'd changed the path you traveled down. Your distance from danger may seem appropriate now, but if you can still see the dog and hear the intimidating growl, you are too close for comfort. Sin is crouching at the door, eager to engage you. So, turn away and go down a different road.

Make no mistake about it. Leashes will break, and dogs like this one will bite.

PROVERBS 22:3-5 (NASB)

"The prudent sees the evil and hides himself, but the naive go on, and are punished for it. The reward of humility and the fear of the Lord are riches, honor and life. Thorns and snares are in the way of the perverse; He who guards himself will be far from them."

position

pore & paraphrase

pull

pose

plan

"Prudent" is from the original Hebrew word aruwm *and means shrewd, sensible.*[1]

"Naïve" is translated from the original Hebrew word pâthiy *and means simple, foolish, open-minded.*[2]

2 TIMOTHY 2:22-26 (ESV)

"So flee youthful passions and pursue righteousness, faith, love, and peace, along with those who call on the LORD from a pure heart. Have nothing to do with foolish, ignorant controversies; you know that they breed quarrels. And the Lord's servant must not be quarrelsome but kind to everyone, able to teach, patiently enduring evil, correcting his opponents with gentleness. God may perhaps grant them repentance leading to a knowledge of the truth, and they may come to their senses and escape from the snare of the devil, after being captured by him to do his will."

position

pore & paraphrase

pull

pose

plan

PSALM 1:1-3 (HCSB)

"How happy is the man who does not follow the advice of the wicked, or take the path of sinners, or join a group of mockers! Instead, his delight is in the LORD's instruction, and he meditates on it day and night. He is like a tree planted beside streams of water that bears its fruit in season and whose leaf does not wither. Whatever he does prospers."

position

pore & paraphrase

pull

pose

plan

Consider the progression of "following the advice" to "taking the path" to "joining a group."

The original language rendered "streams of water" most likely referred to the favored mode of irrigation in some Middle East countries. Canals were dug in many directions; through these the water was carried to all vegetation. The yielding of fruit was dependent on careful navigation and consistent operation of these systems.

"If a person meditates on God's Word, his actions will be godly, and his God-controlled activities will prosper, that is, come to their divinely directed fulfillment."[3]

2 SAMUEL 11:1-4 (NLT)

"In the spring of the year, when kings normally go out to war, David sent Joab and the Israelite army to fight the Ammonites. They destroyed the Ammonite army and laid siege to the city of Rabbah. However, David stayed behind in Jerusalem. Late one afternoon, after his midday rest, David got out of bed and was walking on the roof of the palace. As he looked out over the city, he noticed a woman of unusual beauty taking a bath. He sent someone to find out who she was, and he was told, 'She is Bathsheba, the daughter of Eliam and the wife of Uriah the Hittite.' Then David sent messengers to get her; and when she came to the palace, he slept with her."

Circle the key words from each verse that show the progression in David's sin. Consider how he could have reacted differently at each of these critical stages in order to stop the progression.

GENESIS 19:15-17,26 (NIV)

"With the coming of dawn, the angels urged Lot, saying, 'Hurry! Take your wife and your two daughters who are here, or you will be swept away when the city is punished.' When he hesitated, the men grasped his hand and the hands of his wife and of his two daughters and led them safely out of the city, for the LORD was merciful to them. As soon as they had brought them out, one of them said, 'Flee for your lives! Don't look back, and don't stop anywhere in the plain! Flee to the mountains or you will be swept away!' … But Lot's wife looked back, and she became a pillar of salt."

Lot "hesitated" and his wife "looked back." Consider and compare their reactions to that of Christians and the church today.

"You adulterous people, don't you know that friendship with the world is hatred toward God? Anyone who chooses to be a friend of the world becomes an enemy of God" (Jas. 4:4, NIV).

"Sodom and Gomorrah were a part of a region that was known for its wickedness before God and at the same time admired for its fruitfulness in vegetation. This lush vegetation was enough to attract settlers."[4]

JEREMIAH 6:16 (HCSB)

"This is what the LORD says: Stand by the roadways and look. Ask about the ancient paths: Which is the way to what is good? Then take it and find rest for yourselves. But they protested: 'We won't!'"

position

pore & paraphrase

pull

pose

plan

The "ancient paths" were a reference to the Mosaic law that required morality, holiness, obedience, and compassion.

"Come to Me, all of you who are weary and burdened, and I will give you rest" (Matt. 11:28, HCSB).

1 PETER 5:6-9 (AMP)

"Therefore humble yourselves [demote, lower yourselves in your own estimation] under the mighty hand of God, that in due time He may exalt you, Casting the whole of your care [all your anxieties, all your worries, all your concerns, once and for all] on Him, for He cares for you affectionately and cares about you watchfully. Be well balanced (temperate, sober of mind), be vigilant and cautious at all times; for that enemy of yours, the devil, roams around like a lion roaring [in fierce hunger], seeking someone to seize upon and devour. Withstand him; be firm in faith [against his onset—rooted, established, strong, immovable, and determined], knowing that the same (identical) sufferings are appointed to your brotherhood (the whole body of Christians) throughout the world."

position

pore & paraphrase

pull

pose

plan

Devil *is a Greek word meaning "slanderer." In his role of undermining faith the Devil slanders God to men (Gen. 3:1, 4-5) and men to God (Job 1:9-11; 2:4-5).*

The Message translates "Withstand him" this way—"Keep your guard up." What are some practical ways you can accomplish this?

ROMANS 6:12-13 (NASB)

"Therefore do not let sin reign in your mortal body so that you obey its lusts, and do not go on presenting the members of your body to sin as instruments of unrighteousness; but present yourselves to God as those alive from the dead, and your members as instruments of righteousness to God."

What do you think it means to present the "members of your body" to God?

1 PETER 2:9-12 (NASB)

"But you are A CHOSEN RACE, A ROYAL PRIESTHOOD, A HOLY NATION, A PEOPLE FOR GOD'S OWN POSSESSION, so that you may proclaim the excellencies of Him who has called you out of darkness into His marvelous light; for you once were NOT A PEOPLE, but now you are THE PEOPLE OF GOD; you had NOT RECEIVED MERCY, but now you have RECEIVED MERCY. Beloved, I urge you as aliens and strangers to abstain from fleshly lusts which wage war against the soul. Keep your behavior excellent among the Gentiles, so that in the thing in which they slander you as evildoers, they may because of your good deeds, as they observe them, glorify God in the day of visitation."

position

pore & paraphrase

pull

pose

plan

GENESIS 39:7-12 (HCSB)

"After some time his master's wife looked longingly at Joseph and said, 'Sleep with me.' But he refused. 'Look,' he said to his master's wife, 'with me my master does not concern himself with anything in his house, and he has put all that he owns under my authority. No one in this house is greater than I am. He has withheld nothing from me except you, because you are his wife. So how could I do such a great evil and sin against God?' Although she spoke to Joseph day after day, he refused to go to bed with her. Now one day he went into the house to do his work, and none of the household servants were there. She grabbed him by his garment and said, 'Sleep with me!' But leaving his garment in her hand, he escaped and ran outside."

position
pore & paraphrase
pull
pose
plan

MORE SEEDS
Psalm 119:30; Job 28:28; Psalm 34:14; Psalm 119:101; 1 Corinthians 6:18; 2 Corinthians 6:17;
1 Timothy 6:11; 2 Timothy 2:22

PERSPECTIVES

DVD SESSION: GLORY

> "On the first day of the week Mary Magdalene came early to the tomb, while it was still dark."
> —John 20:1, NASB

3:48 a.m.

That was the time when God spoke.

A digital clock glowed on the screen at the front of the plane. A map displayed the continents and oceans we were flying over. A miniature airplane and a red line charted our progress across the world. We were somewhere between London and Johannesburg—that's all I knew for sure. I was excited about getting to Africa to see this land I'd only known in pictures. Yet, still thousands of miles away, I was already enjoying myself.

Living in a house filled with the excitement of small children, ringing phones, dinner dishes, and an unending to-do list, I was captivated by the stillness and uninterrupted silence this flight provided. When my husband first told me we'd probably spend 20 hours in the air, I was pleased and thankful for a long block of time with no demands, interruptions, or loud noises. Hours into our trip, I was relishing every moment.

I heard no noises but the occasional clacking of the flight attendants' heels in the aisle. Jerry had just downed his last cup of hot tea and was now nestled under the thin, airline-issued blanket. The sun had long taken its leave from the western sky, offering a golden sealed invitation to rest for those aboard the massive bird. The night sky looked like a thick velvety blanket with tiny sequins glistening in starlight glory.

I knew I should sleep to prepare my body for the time change, but I couldn't. I was enjoying these moments too much. The silence was too engaging and offered me a unique opportunity to fully embrace every peaceful second. So I kept my eyes open and relished the experience. How glad I am that I did ... because at 3:48 a.m., God spoke.

I looked out the window at the darkened heavens. The deep, dark abyss of the galaxies beckoned me to commune with Him. I talked. I worshiped. I listened. I listened and then ... He spoke. Not audibly but obviously.

At 3:47 we entered a tuft of clouds as the pilot ascended to a different altitude. For only a few seconds we were lost in the blanket of billowing whiteness. When the plane burst out the other side, I was blinded. The sun, unseen and unknown moments before, became fully exposed. The wings of the spacious sky carried the brilliance of each robust ray of light, delivering each color of the spectrum to the oval windows of every row. The sun was shining with blinding opulence.

My hands leapt to cover my eyes. I had no choice but turn and look away. My gaze into the plane lasted long enough to notice many passengers were just as shocked by the bright light as I. They were turning over, putting on sleeping masks, and closing their window shades. I watched, for a while, everyone adjusting. And that's when I saw ... the clock ... 3:48 a.m.

Everyone was taken aback by the stark light. I had my eyes shaded by the palm of my hand. We were all smack dab in the presence of the dazzling and vivid robust sun, and yet it was 3:48 in the morning.

How could it be 3 o'clock in the morning? Hours so close to midnight never looked like this before. I'd heard of the arctic dwellers experiencing this phenomenon but never thought I'd see the wee hours like this. I was completely floored by the appearance of 3:48 a.m. from this vantage point.

I guess how you see midnight hours all depends on the perspective from which you take them in.

Perspectives
What's yours regarding your husband? your children? your mother? your job? your house? today? tomorrow? I admit that entire seasons of my life have carried the typical darkness the 3 a.m. time frame normally depicts.

From my vantage point, singlehood was too long, then marriage too hard, and children too much work. From this angle, ministry is laborious and the details of life too meticulous and demanding. Isn't that what the cloud cover of discontentment always does? Looking at life from this angle always seems to lend itself to the darkest possible version.

So we sit in the dark, thinking that life will get brighter when circumstances change. We are completely unaware that the glorious beauty of God's plan and purposes are displayed even when ... especially when ... darkness is on the flip side.

So what can we say to ...
The woman whose husband has revealed his affair
The husband who's loving an alcoholic wife
The parent whose child was lost in an accident
The worker whose inbox just received a pink slip
The newlywed whose doctor says pregnancy is impossible
The teenager who's not wanted in the clique
The woman who births a special needs child
The friend that just found out she's been betrayed in the worst possible way

Why did God—how could God—have allowed it? Really, no rational answer exists. We'll most likely never fully understand. So until we see Him face to face, we must turn our perspective to take in the best possible view of these opaque days, to see them from God's vantage point, and to relish His work in the wee hours.

Mary knew about the dark. That's what it was when she arrived at the tomb on the first day of the week (John 20:1). From her perspective, she could imagine no horror worse than the one she beheld. She saw insult piled on top of injury. Before her lay an empty tomb. The stone had been rolled away, and the broken body of her Lord was gone. She wept in anguish (John 20:11) and longed for that which it seemed she could not have. But then she heard her name, "Mary." Her name only rolled off of the tongue in that way from One person. So "she turned around " (John 20:14).

Hear that again. She turned around ... She turned ... around ...

Her newly focused gaze brought her face to face with the brilliance and the beauty of the risen Christ. What had just been empty was made full with one small but deliberate movement. A simple change of perspective changed her life.

This day I ask you to turn around—to turn your face away from the empty. I ask you to turn to the full, away from the dark and to the blinding light. I pray that God calls your name with such sweetness and authority in the midst of the darkness that you will not be able to help but see His face in your circumstances. A decision to change your perspective, my friend, can change your whole life.

May we be lifted by the wings of the Spirit through the clouds of contempt and complacency so that our eyes behold the greatest of this day and the rest of our lives. AMEN

PSALM 23:1-6 (NET)

"The LORD is my shepherd, I lack nothing. He takes me to lush pastures, he leads me to refreshing water. He restores my strength. He leads me down the right paths for the sake of his reputation. Even when I must walk through the darkest valley, I fear no danger, for you are with me; your rod and your staff reassure me. You prepare a feast before me in plain sight of my enemies. You refresh my head with oil; my cup is completely full. Surely your goodness and faithfulness will pursue me all my days, and I will live in the LORD's house for the rest of my life."

The good shepherds of the Near East in the time when David lived would never leave their flock. They were ever present and fully aware of the situations occurring in the lives of their sheep.

What might be some reasons why a sheep might not be able to see his shepherd?

The rod was a heavy club the shepherd used to kill predators, and the staff, a long pole with a crook in one end, used to round up the sheep and to guide them along.

The sight of those instruments caused David to realize that he had absolutely nothing to fear. His shepherd was there to kill the enemies of fear, doubt, and guilt and to guide him safely through.[1]

ISAIAH 43:1-2 (NLT)

From the Lord to Israel facing the long journey
home from exile to rebuild the temple

"But now, O Jacob, listen to the LORD who created you. O Israel, the one who formed you says, 'Do not be afraid, for I have ransomed you. I have called you by name; you are mine. When you go through deep waters, I will be with you. When you go through rivers of difficulty, you will not drown. When you walk through the fire of oppression, you will not be burned up; the flames will not consume you.'"

A reoccurring theme in this section of the book of Isaiah is "Fear Not!" It is said seven times in this section alone.

This passage begins with the words "But now," thereby relating it to the preceding statement. This connection is important as the prophet now turns from the past to the future.

Why do you think that God may allow one to "walk through the fire" or be positioned near "flames"?

DANIEL 3:20-25 (NASB)

"He [King Nebuchadnezzar] commanded certain valiant warriors who were in his army to tie up Shadrach, Meshach and Abed-nego in order to cast them into the furnace of blazing fire. Then these men were tied up in their trousers, their coats, their caps and their other clothes, and were cast into the midst of the furnace of blazing fire. For this reason, because the king's command was urgent and the furnace had been made extremely hot, the flame of the fire slew those men who carried up Shadrach, Meshach and Abed-nego. But these three men, Shadrach, Meshach and Abed-nego, fell into the midst of the furnace of blazing fire still tied up. Then Nebuchadnezzar the king was astounded and stood up in haste; he said to his high officials, 'Was it not three men we cast bound into the midst of the fire?' They replied to the king, 'Certainly, O king.' He said, 'Look! I see four men loosed and walking about in the midst of the fire without harm, and the appearance of the fourth is like a son of the gods!'"

position
pore & paraphrase
pull
pose
plan

What circumstances have you been facing that seem to be intensifying in difficulty?

What significance might there be to the fact that they went into the furnace bound but became unbound while in it?

In what ways have you seen freedom result personally from life's trials?

ROMANS 8:35,37-59 (HCSB)

"Who can separate us from the love of Christ? Can affliction or anguish or persecution or famine or nakedness or danger or sword? ... No, in all these things we are more than victorious through Him who loved us. For I am persuaded that not even death nor life, angels or rulers, things present or things to come, hostile powers, height or depth, or any other created thing will have the power to separate us from the love of God that is in Christ Jesus our Lord!"

Affliction (thlipsis) distress brought on by outward circumstances.

Anguish (stenochoria) torturing confinement, hemmed in with no way out.[2]

Persecution (diogmos) a program or process designed to harass and oppress someone.[2]

How does the knowledge of Christ's unending love help you to remain victorious in the midst of trying circumstances?

ISAIAH 55:8-13 (NLT)

"'My thoughts are nothing like your thoughts,' says the Lord. 'And my ways are far beyond anything you could imagine. For just as the heavens are higher than the earth, so my ways are higher than your ways and my thoughts higher than your thoughts. The rain and snow come down from the heavens and stay on the ground to water the earth. They cause the grain to grow, producing seed for the farmer and bread for the hungry. It is the same with my word. I send it out, and it always produces fruit. It will accomplish all I want it to, and it will prosper everywhere I send it. You will live in joy and peace. The mountains and hills will burst into song, and the trees of the field will clap their hands! Where once there were thorns, cypress trees will grow. Where nettles grew, myrtles will sprout up. These events will bring great honor to the Lord's name; they will be an everlasting sign of his power and love.'"

The original word for "thoughts" does not reference understanding but points more to the creating of new ideas. The way God creates and executes ideas is completely different than the way humans would.

In the Near East dry, hard ground can seemingly overnight sprout with vegetation after the first rains of the rainy season. Similarly when God speaks His Word, it brings forth spiritual life, thus ac-complishing His purpose. [3]

GENESIS 45:4-8 (HCSB)

"Then Joseph said to his brothers, 'Please, come near me,' and they came near. 'I am Joseph, your brother,' he said, 'the one you sold into Egypt. And now don't be worried or angry with yourselves for selling me here, because God sent me ahead of you to preserve life. For the famine has been in the land these two years, and there will be five more years without plowing or harvesting. God sent me ahead of you to establish you as a remnant within the land and to keep you alive by a great deliverance. Therefore it was not you who sent me here, but God. He has made me a father to Pharaoh, lord of his entire household, and ruler over all the land of Egypt.'"

position

pore & paraphrase

pull

pose

plan

Chronicle the many different difficulties that were
faced by the individuals
involved. Consider God's
perspective on each one
and how it might have
been vastly different than
theirs.

Genesis 50:19-20 (NASB)

COLOSSIANS 3:1-2 (AMP)

"IF THEN you have been raised with Christ [to a new life, thus sharing His resurrection from the dead], aim at and seek the [rich, eternal treasures] that are above, where Christ is, seated at the right hand of God. And set your minds and keep them set on what is above (the higher things), not on the things that are on the earth."

Make special note of the directives given by Paul. Circle the verbs that specify what the Christian is to do and consider how you can best facilitate this in your own life.

How have you seen that setting your mind on heavenly things has changed how you viewed earthly things and vice versa? How might setting your mind on earthly things make it harder for you to see God?

PHILIPPIANS 4:8 (NASB)

"Finally, brethren, whatever is true, whatever is honorable, whatever is right, whatever is pure, whatever is lovely, whatever is of good repute, if there is any excellence and if anything worthy of praise, dwell on these things."

True (alethe) things are the opposite of dishonest and unreliable things (Eph. 4:15,25).

Noble refers to what is dignified and worthy of respect.

Right (dikaia) refers to conformity to God's standards.

Pure (hagna) refers to what is wholesome, not mixed with moral impurity.

Lovely speaks of what promotes peace rather than conflict.

Admirable relates to what is positive and constructive rather than negative and destructive.[4]

PHILIPPIANS 4:11-13 (HCSB)

Paul to the believers at Philippi who were concerned about his needs

"I don't say this out of need, for I have learned to be content in whatever circumstances I am. I know both how to have a little, and I know how to have a lot. In any and all circumstances I have learned the secret of being content—whether well-fed or hungry, whether in abundance or in need. I am able to do all things through Him who strengthens me."

The root word translated "secret" literally means to learn the secret of something by initiation.[5] Paul was saying that his experiences, both in abasement and abundance, were his initiation into the knowledge of the great mystery of contentment.

GENESIS 28:12,16-19 (NASB)

Jacob's dream

"Behold, a ladder was set on the earth with its top reaching to heaven; and behold, the angels of God were ascending and descending on it. ... Then Jacob awoke from his sleep and said, 'Surely the LORD is in this place, and I did not know it.' He was afraid and said, 'How awesome is this place! This is none other than the house of God, and this is the gate of heaven.' So Jacob rose early in the morning, and took the stone that he had put under his head and set it up as a pillar and poured oil on its top. He called the name of that place Bethel; however, previously the name of the city had been Luz."

"The dream assured Jacob that despite his deceit he was the corridor of the blessings of the Abrahamic covenant."[6]

Recall a time when God graciously revealed Himself to you despite any disobedience and rebellion. How did this experience cause you to respond to Him in the future?

The name Bethel *means "House of God."*

MORE SEEDS
Deuteronomy 8:15-16; Nahum 1:7; Colossians 3:2; Jeremiah 29:11; Romans 11:33; Romans 8:28; Ephesians 1:11; Genesis 39:20-21; 2 Corinthians 4:16-17; Romans 5:3-5; Romans 8:28-30; 1 Peter 1:6-7; 2 Corinthians 1:3-6; 2 Corinthians 4:8; Habbakuk 3:17-19; Esther 4:14; Philippians 1:12-14

LEADER GUIDE

Thank you for leading a Seed Bible study group. Here is some information you might find useful:

1. The two Seed studies include six Seed DVD's. Each contains a modern-day parable on video and a list of discussion questions. You can purchase them individually and use them to foster a one-time Bible study discussion or simply use the DVD presentation as an enhancement for an event or meeting.
2. For on-going meetings, we've combined the DVD's into two packs—three in each pack. Each set covers three weeks of meetings. Seed Pack 1 and Seed Pack 2 both contain three video parables, each presenting a different theme, and one member book for the leader.
3. Individual members will need to purchase their own member book to enhance their participation in this study. Additionally, the books can be used without their accompanying DVD session for individuals or groups that prefer the print only.

At your first meeting explain:
1. This study is unlike others. Each week will present a different theme.
2. This study is designed to stimulate conversation with God through Scripture to become more personal and will be worth their effort. Some thoughts that I share in the introduction may help you with this.
3. Introduce the "5 P" method, using my description from pages 7-11. Familiarizing yourself with this process will help you explain it and answer any questions.

Watch the DVD and use the discussion questions to stir the conversation. Before you conclude your meeting, remind participants to use the "5 P" method to continue their conversation with God for the remainder of the week. Explain that there is no homework to finish or problems to solve—just Scripture to meditate on. Encourage them to select one passage each day. I've purposefully given more Scripture than necessary in hopes that this resource can be used again.

When your group reconvenes the following week, allot some time for members to share what they sensed the Lord saying to them from the passages they reviewed. After the designated time, watch the next video in the series and start the process for the following week. Thank you for your diligence in serving God's people. I am praying for you.

Blessings, Priscilla

DISCUSSION QUESTIONS

ARMOR
Background Scripture:
Ephesians 6:10-18

1. Sometimes we live as if the enemy doesn't exist. In what areas of your life have you let down your guard?
2. How can remembering you have an enemy change the way you live?
3. In what ways have you noticed the enemy trying to thwart your progress lately?
4. What do you think he is trying to keep you from accomplishing?
5. How have his attempts intimidated you or caused you to back down from your purpose?
6. What are the differences between following God's will while guarding against enemy attacks vs. going into a bad situation thinking God will protect you?
7. Consider the armor of God passage (Eph. 6) and contemplate how each piece can be used practically in the life of a believer.
8. What are you currently doing to protect yourself against the enemy's attacks?
9. What aren't you doing that you need to begin taking seriously?
10. How will being aware of the enemy's hand behind occurrences in the physical realm cause you to adjust your reaction?

FIVE

**Background Scripture:
Romans 7:13–8:13**

1. How would you interpret the visual metaphors in the video—hole in sidewalk, faucet running, and so forth?
2. What is your normal way of responding when you "fall in a hole"?
3. What does Priscilla's statement mean to you: "The light of day has never looked so bright as when glaring in the eyes of someone who has been acquainted with the darkness"?
4. Why do you think we sometimes stay in the hole longer than necessary? What makes getting out of the hole so difficult?
5. If you can share, what pitfalls or holes do you find yourself falling into repeatedly?
6. How do you relate to Paul's statements in Romans 7:15-17, 25; 8:11?
7. What is the difference between conviction and condemnation (Rom. 8:1)?
8. How do we come back to our senses? Or, how do we move from chapter 3 to chapter 4?
9. What part does the Lord play in getting you out of your hole? What part do you play?
10. Do you believe God has new chapters for your story? How can you live in response to God's promise in Philippians 1:6?

DISCUSSION QUESTIONS
GLORY
Background Scripture:
John 1:14-17

1. What circumstances in your life have made it difficult to detect that God's presence is with you?
2. As you look more carefully, how can God's hand now be recognized?
3. How close does someone have to get to your life before he or she sees God?
4. The scriptural examples that Priscilla references are not the best of circumstances (Jesus on the cross, Hagar in distress, the Israelites in the wilderness). Are you willing to see God at work even when He will be best seen in something that causes you discomfort?
5. How can you make it a practice to look for God in the regular, everyday rhythm of your life?
6. Discuss the statement: "If you change your perspective from broad to intimate, you'll see that there's much more to be seen."
7. Why is it easier to see God working in broad brushstrokes throughout time rather than intimately involved in our lives?
8. How have you seen His hand beckoning, granting, forgiving, encouraging, comforting?
9. In what specific way has God changed your perspective on something you feel strongly about?

ENDNOTES

Session 1

1. John F. Walvoord, Roy B. Zuck, *The Bible Knowledge Commentary: An Exposition of the Scriptures* (Wheaton, IL: Victor Books, 1983), 750.

Session 2

1. James Strong, *Strong's Exhaustive Concordance of the Bible* (Peabody, MA: Hendrickson Publishers, n.d.), 6175.
2. Ibid., 6612.
3. John F. Walvoord, Roy B. Zuck, *The Bible Knowledge Commentary: An Exposition of the Scriptures* (Wheaton, IL: Victor Books, 1983), 790.
4. Walter L. Elwell, *Baker Encyclopedia of the Bible* (Ada, MI: Baker Publishing Group, 1997), 466.

Session 3

1. R. Ellsworth, *Opening up Psalms* (Leominster: Day One Publications, 2006), 49.
2. Cleon L. Rogers, Jr. and Cleon Rogers, *The New Linguistic and Exegetical Key to the Greek New Testament* (Grand Rapids, MI: Zondervan, 1998), 319.
3. John F. Walvoord, Roy B. Zuck, *The Bible Knowledge Commentary: An Exposition of the Scriptures* (Wheaton, IL: Victor Books, 1983).
4. Ibid., 664.
5. Kurt Aland, *Greek-English Lexicon of the New Testament* (elec. edition) (New York: United Bible Societies, 1998).
6. J. M. Freeman and H. J. Chadwick, *Manners and Customs of the Bible* (North Brunswick, NJ: Bridge-Logos Publishers, 1998), 49.